On the Mountain

On the Mountain

Alan Archer Stephens

Copyright © 2024 by Alan Archer Stephens

All rights reserved
Printed in the United States of America

Cover photo: Alan Archer Stephens
VAL Books, Port Townsend WA
Set in Sabon Next. Book title set in Hiroshige.

ISBN 978-0-9973923-2-6 (paper)

to Valerie
sine qua non

Contents

fog sleeps over the bay	3
early mornings	4
neighborhood lights sharpen	5
above the hills in early light	6
conga beats	7
On the Mountain	8
This week I spoke	9
A Peach at a Year and a Half	10
Young Man	11
Athena Biblioteka	12
El Capitán	13
Freeways	14
New Path	15
On the Mountain II	16
Hawk	18
July 21, 2009	19
Fran's Dream: December 2011	20
Ashes	22
Ashes II	24
Visit	26
Thirty-Nine Pelicans	28
On the Mountain III — Big Wind	29
A Lushih for John R.	31
Homage to Emily Bronte	32
Han Yu	33
Homage to Peter Josheff	34
Age Before Beauty	35
Op. 11, B-flat Major	36
Hospital Doors	37

Donna	38
On the Mountain IV—The Mermaid	39
Eyes	40
Ignis Mundi	41
Approaching Fall	42
October	44
Year End	45
On the Mountain V	46
Not That Into Us	47
What Is	48
Apperception	49
I look up	50
Only I	51
The Extent of It	52
Angenga	53
Trails	54
Boink!	55
Problem Is It Makes a Mess	56
Solstice Ferry	57
On the Mountain VI	58
This Egret	59
On the Ridge	60
West Marin	61
Elephant Mountain	62
Drake's Beach	63
On the Bluff	64
Abbotts Lagoon	65
Destination	66
On the Mountain VII	67
Early at the Mission	68
Dawn at Carmel River	69
So Happened	70
Otters	71
Ancient Harvester	72

River	73
Red Abalone	74
Cavalry	75
On the Mountain VIII	76
Clipper Cove	77
Driving In	78
The Spiders	79
A Full Moon Through Binoculars	80
A Dream	81
Asilomar	83
January Thought	84
On the Mountain IX	85
Autumn Lights	86
End of November	87
12.19.22	88
Passage	89
The plum doesn't know	90
End of February	91
On the Mountain X	92
The Rain	94
Gnomon	95
Buddhas	96
Green and Gold	97
West Berkeley	98
Surely the Rain	99
Home three days	100
Uno Día Más	101

Translations

Horace
Book I, Ode XI (Don't ask what end)	103
Book I, Ode XVIII (Plant no tree)	104
Book I, Ode XXXIV (Never one for piety)	105

- Book II, Ode I (Pollio, ...) — 106
- Book II, Ode XV (Sailors caught on the open sea) — 108
- Book II, Ode XXI (You were born with me) — 110
- Book III, Ode XXII (Diana, ...) — 111
- Book IV, Ode VII (The snow is gone) — 112

Tu Fu
- Jade Flower Palace — 113
- To Wei Pa — 114
- Coming Home at Night — 115
- Facing Snow — 116
- Leaving the City — 117
- Standing Alone — 118
- At a Meeting of Rivers — 119
- Night Thoughts Traveling — 120

Wang Wei
- Deer Park — 121

Li Po
- Fragment (I wake from a dream) — 122

Su Tung-P'o
- Fragment (Don't mind the beat of the rain) — 123
- The Wind — 124

Lu Yu
- Thoughts Passing a Farm House — 125

About the Author — 127

On the Mountain

fog sleeps over the bay
a demon watches at the gate
perhaps there is another way
along the wall to slip by fate

early mornings
the crows and I are active

they seem to know
what they're up to

neighborhood lights sharpen
beneath a dawn sky Grizzly Peak
wears a brooch of bright diamonds
on the breast of her black velvet dress

above the hills in early light
a silver saucer, perfectly level
snugly holds her darkened globe
beside the morning star

crescent so slender and sharp
planet so self-contained —
heaven's table brilliantly set

1.26.21

conga beats
on my coffee lid

rain pelting the beach
wind piling up foam

just me and the geese
out here at dawn

Carmel River State Beach

On the Mountain

Northwest a sparsely settled coast
and the vast wild ocean

Southeast the cities of the bay
in their sink of urban air

Bridges and highways span the sprawl
so cars and trucks can crawl
around the glittering water

The stink of human progress stands
beside the beautiful boundaries of the land.

This week I spoke
to a deer, a lizard,
several dogs, a couple of cats,
a few towhees, and some crows.
Surely they didn't know
what I was saying
but they got the drift.
Even the lizard scrambled
off the trail when I told him
it would be a good idea.

A Peach at a Year and a Half

He reaches out from his perch
    in the shopping cart

Gently, he feels the fur
    on the orange globe

Carefully, with little fingers
    he grasps and lifts it

Young Man

He's around six, just out
of the family car on
Berkeley Way at Bonita.

He turns and delivers
a series of karate strikes
just short of the car door,

and then, as his calm mother
and unimpressed little brother
head down to Trader Joe's,

he does a little dance
holstering his hands
those lethal weapons

and lifting his knees
the way boys do
producing in a passerby

an echo of his joy.

Athena Biblioteka

She presides over the entrance
Three steeds charging atop her helmet
Gorgoneion on her breastplate
Open-mouthed in horror

The goddess herself however
Is nearly expressionless
In blank eyes and divine face
Serene inhuman determination

El Capitán

The big waves came in late summer
we rode them in, immersed in their collapse
spun under sometimes, tumbled on the bottom
thrashed and glad to stumble up the beach
bitter taste of brine in the throat.

After sunset on the cooling sand
headlights swinging down from Gaviota
the mystery and possibility of the world
mountains close against the sea—
who knew what sets were yet to come?

Freeways

Heading into LA from OC on a Sunday morning
and traffic is light, reminding me that I love
driving a freeway at speed, the way it should be.

Southern California raised, I like to go places fast
in my car, eighty miles an hour is the god-given right
of Californians if the flow permits, and one we share gladly

with fellow travelers from outside the state, unfortunate
souls who have to live somewhere other than this
freeway heaven, even if it sometimes seems like hell.

Northern Californian now, I think how much easier
it is to navigate the labyrinth with the directions lady
on the phone telling me what to do next … nagging me even.

Before these cheating phones we drove one time to Irvine
to visit our son. In traffic I took two wrong freeway turns by mistake
and one on misguided purpose. Three hours into the miasma

we were on the right freeway at last, when all the lanes
shut down because a guy was about to jump into traffic
from a pedestrian bridge. Dude, I thought, I get it, but still.

Finally ensconced in our American Generic OC lodging
we ate In-N-Out burgers and drank Chateauneuf-du-Pape
from Trader Joe's. California life, wouldn't trade it for anything.

New Path

Down to the end of the street and up
the stairs, then left across the basketball court
bag in hand, alert for a chance to pick up
the trash that accumulates there, the sort
you see everywhere, but this little stretch
is my chosen patrol. Then up the trail
to the station where I, no longer a wretch
bound to his commute, peel off and sail
up Virginia. I hit my pace and stride
the pleasant neighborhood. A hill at the top
and more stairs, where a lion face presides,
spirit of an unkempt grove. There I stop
and turn for the grand bay view, before proceeding
to the hall in Doe to resume, at last, my reading.

7.2.18

On the Mountain II

The twisting drive up through Mill Valley
gains the ridge above Muir Woods,
winds in and out of forest
(window down for the conifer scent),
climbs out of trees onto tawny slopes
dotted with clumps of dark bay and oak,
and ends at the western parking lot.

The trail leads past a cluster of tables
in a clearing backed by woods, and out
onto the high open flank of Tamalpais
overlooking the coast northwest—
Stinson, Bolinas, Point Reyes, the Farallons
out in the ocean. On such a day as this
everything gleams in soft morning sunlight,
fishing boats off Stinson, the lagoon
and forested bluff of Bolinas, the pale cliffs
on the curve of Drake's Bay, the little islands
so lonely in the sea that extends
huge to the horizon.

I visit my favorite group of boulders and bays
maintaining their air of mystery in full sun,
then head over to O'Rourke's Bench, that kingly seat
with views of the gate, the city, the enormous bay,
and looming over the East Bay Hills, Diablo,
the big mountain. This one here is the elegant one,
pretty in profile, showing some skin
on certain hillsides, stylishly revealed.

I cannot drink my fill of this day and place,
it's too big, I'm too small.
I make my way to the last wooded knoll
where the oak in whose hollow trunk
my young self used to shelter is now fallen,
beginning the process of returning
to earth. A place rooted in memory.
A tour of these little woods, a last look eastward
then back along the ridge-top trail.
A final draft of the view up the coast,
and I'm back at the car.

Not another soul on the trails, and mine,
a bit battered of late, tottering along
on creaky knees, is grateful to be here,
determined to return to be again
on the mountain in the big mix.

Hawk

Morning in the front yard
a sudden commotion of leaves
and feathers bursting through
the big oak's canopy.

There he is, a red-tail
perched on a thick limb
huge and haughty, glaring about
with a glance my way.

Old as I am, I find myself
thinking, "Dad?"

July 21, 2009

A mild morning—summer was never for you,
child of December dark, of clear
cold nights, maybe a thin rim
of moon descending early—now
in the off-season, sons gathered
for your final days—what do we know?
Not much, you're seeing things beyond
our ken, walking a strange path
to the exit. So it's happened,
and the family is glad to be here together,
five as we were in the beginning,
as we are at the end, ready as we can be.

I drop a dose of morphine into your mouth, then
go up and start a stream of Bach
on the stereo. Goldberg Variations—
the opening aria plays as I return
to your room, where the sun
filters through oaks, and the notes
trickle through dining room and kitchen
down to where you lie. No sign you chose
this time but it came, quietly.
And who knows? Maybe you took the chance
to leave with a masterpiece.

Fran's Dream: December 2011

She was a circus performer
in a motorcycle act. She had a "premonition,"
so she and the man who was her partner
"drafted" a monkey and rode away.

They took their show on the road,
and something bad did happen
at the circus, and people were hurt.
They decided to send the monkey back,

then boarded a train, but
she had an "inclination" that something
would happen, so they got off,
and something bad did happen.

So, she said, her instincts saved her again.

Perhaps her mind was seeking
escapes from her firm commitment
to keep ALS from having its fatal way
with her body, once so full of grace

and energy, a fittingly lovely frame
for a beautifully capable woman.
Mind clear and spirit strong, she fasted
without complaint to reach her end.

Dozing off on the last morning
she said "I'm adding to my motorcycle story."
She spent years tending our father
in his decline. But before that long catastrophe,

the dream might say, she rode as a poet's wife.

Ashes

I saved some of each of your ashes
in little jars, intending to combine them
in an appropriate receptacle.

Years passed. Then in the factory store
of Heath Ceramics, my wife
reminded me of that plan

and there was a piece, quite small,
a matchstick holder, but suitably elegant—
cylindrical, brown, a finish like fine leather.

At home I brought the jars out
from a corner of my cabinet.
They sat on a shelf with the new container

for a few days. It made me sad,
and when I took them out back to put a few
teaspoons from each in the cylinder,

it was sadder than I ever imagined.
There are ashes left over. I'll pour them
into a river running to the sea.

They're not who you were, not
the people we children remember.
But the elegant little brown cylinder

will do as a token of those lives
spent well together. For us
admiration runs with sorrow.

9.4.18

Ashes II

A foggy dawn at high tide, and the little river
runs swiftly to the surf, pushing up crests
when it hits broken waves, surging over the ebb,
persistently vanishing into the sea, without remorse.
Standing beside it, where the last ledges
of ocean foam sink into sand, I open
the two little jars and tip them with a shake.

Mom, yours slid out clean as a whistle
a gray plume instantly slipping downstream.
Dad, yours stuck, only a bit breaking loose
and a big wave lapped over my boots
as I scooped up water and shook.
Four or five times I had to dip and shake
before the jar rinsed clean and the traces slid away.

I look up and a hundred gulls are wheeling above
this confluence, silently soaring and circling.
They drift away to light on the lagoon
but soon take back to the air, swirling over me,
settling on the beach across the river, rising again
to sail above the spot where fresh hits salt,
obsessively riding the wind off the sea.

I walk down the beach, climb up the bluff,
stroll around the point, and on the way back to the car
observe that the gulls are still at it,
patrolling the place where the last of your remains,

but for the teaspoons in the brown cylinder,
were carried by the river to the sea
and mixed past recognition.

Carmel River State Beach, 1.29.19

Visit

No gravestones, no soil under sod
but this stretch of brown sand
washed over and over by waves
riding up and falling back.

Out in the surf where we put
the remains, watch is kept
by the perch, the passing seal,
the occasional dolphin patrol.

When your sons come back
to where they grew up
they can visit this place,
better than a cemetery,

where once they ran, swam,
rode waves, built castles,
warmed skinny selves in the hot sand
after chilling them in the sea.

After they left, your lives
ran their own courses
in the watershed stretching
from here to the mountains.

Now I return, an old man
in February. It's low tide at dawn.
A helmet moon shines in the sky
and on the flat wet sand at my feet.

A curlew trots along nervously
ahead of me, and I'm grateful
for this beautiful plain place,
your resting place that never rests.

Hendry's Beach, 2.13.20

Thirty-Nine Pelicans

for my parents

Slung out in a long line, they swoop
low over the gently lapping surface of
the Channel waters where your ashes floated
briefly, now many years ago, and the line
is a brief formation too as the big birds
bunch up and regroup, sailing along
at speed with just a few wingbeats.

Always in flux, the sea, the air above it,
the sand beside it, the living things
that swim and fly and walk here.
All that is is changing, and I take
my changing place in this May dawn
along this shore, where we had happiness
thanks to you, who are at rest and change no more.

5.12.22

On the Mountain III — Big Wind

Chased me out of my forest revery —
branches and even trunks
lie in ruins around me.
Only an idiot would linger in
his favorite place when
treetops toss and roar like this.

Oddly, downslope the air
is calmer and the forest assumes
its usual glamorous look
as I follow the edge —
who could resist? Not me,
these trees are magic.

Working my way south
around the mountain shoulder
the wind becomes a factor again.
Steep slope, old man, bad knees,
that push is real. Must maintain
balance on the trail.

It leads to a discovery —
the bay leaning over the bench
has lost one of its trunks
in the big wind … it weighs
massively on junior branches.
I snap off a top sprig

to keep the leaves for seasoning
my soups and stews. They must
have magical properties,
right? Not really, but they are
bay leaves and there is
magic in the forests up here.

A Lushih for John R.

Tall warm presence in childhood memory
Happy voice in the old house echoing

Fellow poet and good friend to my father
Friend to me after my father's going

Stricken by family sorrow when young
Still the wit and verse kept flowing

Now this news—you're in the hospital
With an evil guest—is difficult knowing

Homage to Emily Bronte

No coward soul is mine
No fool in thrall to faith
No grasper for a sign
Of immortality, no wraith

Pretending not to die—the vanity
Of all creeds strikes me plain
I cast my lot with sanity
And reap its modest gains,

A clearer view of present things
Oblivion as our sure hereafter
Pleasure in free thinking
New questions and ideas, laughter,

Wine, food, and friends,
The arts and sciences, every
Good thing I can find,
And I find good the reverie

That comes with walking by the sea
The lovely shores of this my place
Bring tides of wonder over me
In this swift life, this human race.

Han Yu

Not the poet that Tu or Li were, but author
of fine verse and prose, you speak to us
skeptics, enemies of superstition embittered
by the evil that flows from human folly.

The leaves spinning down before your door
in autumn dusk, and the words of an ancient poet
fill your heart with grief, but you say
a man must think things through,
there's work to be done, work that never ends.

Exiled for warning the emperor not to get caught
in the excitement at the arrival of a relic—
said to be a finger-bone of the Buddha—
you tell your nephew there must be a reason
he's ridden with you so far, and ask him a favor—
to collect your bones from the swamp by the river.

Of course you were recalled and died in Chang'an.
Your mordant words, though, stretch over centuries.

Homage to Peter Josheff

Among ancients at the noon concert—appearances
can deceive, some are sharp and knowing—
prepared to hear this "modern chamber music"
I absorb vibrations of flute, clarinet, and piano.

It's a musical imagination of fog and mist
of hiking up for a view west over the bay
of sun overhead with Sutro Tower rising from the fog
of floating across the bay to hover above the spires
then plummeting down to the base.

And when the artist turns to the spoken word
accompanied by piano, I marvel at his skill.
Poems pulled off, fitted to the notes,
a work in progress but a man in command
of his materials—a pleasure to behold.

Hertz Hall, 11.24.21

Age Before Beauty

At the concert a crone
creeps to her first row seat
as a nymph sings on stage.

Op. 11, B-flat Major

A while ago this melody was in my head,
an ear-worm but complex, extended.
I searched my collection in vain.
Yesterday at lunch it came on the radio
and I looked it up online (what a thing).
Were I sophisticated I would've suspected
it was Beethoven, but I'm not.
I'd been thinking symphony, but it's not.
So I overlooked this trio
in the CDs my parents left me—
Serkin's Marlboro Festival edition,
1974—a very good year (for me).
A fine rendition of a sinuous piece,
cleverly constructed. You're reminded
with imperious force (it being Beethoven)
what genius can do with its instruments.

Hospital Doors

You're in there after an episode of amnesia
and they kept you overnight for testing.
At last I hear that everything's all right
and I can come get you. No one's around
as I wait outside — covid keeps me from entering.
The doors slide open and out you walk
alone, your old self, smiling self-consciously
as joy lifts my arms overhead
and I walk to you for an embrace.
Joys bloom like flowers, for a time,
but this one will live in memory —
a fragile existence, we've been taught.

12.21.20

Donna

You don't like to look at your face
now that you're in your seventies
but I do. It's beautiful in its brownness,
its Japaneseness, its solid roundness,
and the wrinkles are dear to me
after all these years. Most of all
I love to see it because it means
you're here with me, thank goodness,
for what would I do without you?
I don't like to think about that.

On the Mountain IV — The Mermaid

I find her on a picnic table by the grove, my first station,
a little doll neatly stuffed and sewn. Saffron mane of yarn,
round black eyes, red smile, nipples ribs and sternum
picked out in khaki on her beige torso, curving tail encased
in turquoise and adorned with three fish — orange, yellow, green —
each with three glass beads around its head, for bubbles,
and stretched between them in orange letters her name — *AMOR*.
She seems to be brand new, nary a smudge on her, though
she's been thoroughly soaked by the rains. I leave her on the table
as I make my rounds — maybe a little girl will come to rescue her.
But again I have this marvelous place to myself
so on the way back I pick her up to take home to the little girl
who lives on in my old wife, and loves mermaids.

Eyes

Dark, deep-set, beneath the balding brow
Of a man of years, seated at a desk
Overlooking the harbor, pondering now
In his choice office, the features of a task.

Flashing, wide-open, beneath the fierce brows
Of a toddler on the restaurant deck, not fixed
On parents or sister, but on the birds that arouse
Her wonder—blackbird! seagull! Awe unmixed.

I meet his and there's an understanding
Of sorts, we being the same kind. I meet hers
And realize at once that an old man lunching
Is but a paltry thing next to birds.

In times of social distance, I find, the eyes
Of fellow humans can be a fine surprise.

Ignis Mundi

Smoke chokes the sky—this beautiful place
Is on fire. The red sun casts an evil glow,
Leading the mind to brood, brood on waste,
The desert that was Eden, Rome laid low,
The barren hills of Israel and Greece,
The ugliness of factory and freeway,
Of parking lots, power lines, city streets,
The greed and hate and lies that rule the day.
Destruction haunts the spirit as it wanders
On its paths, even as daily needs are met—
For now, the mind mutters, for the blunders
That brought us here aren't finished, don't forget.
    Fires burn the wilderness, harry settlements,
    Flicker through thoughts, smolder in events.

9.1.20

Approaching Fall

After days of smoke the air is clear,
the afternoon blue, so I take my walk
up Virginia to campus, reveling
in the visibility of the hills,
the little breeze that keeps me cool,
the bank of fog that hangs across the gate,
half hiding the bridge as I look out
From PSR. The fine old buildings here
are a marvel, as are those on campus —
but the library, with its great reading hall,
my temple, is now closed
By the pandemic ... and the reveling subsides.
Still there are the favorite statues,
the saber-tooth cat, the nymph, the pelican.
And the great bell tower, the redwoods,
the running creeks, the old oaks, the grove
of eucalyptus, so tall, the cherry trees
lined up along the entrance drive.

As lovely a day as September provides,
as lovely a place as I could wish
to mourn the disasters of our time —
the fires, revenge of the injured climate,
the pandemic, revenge of the wildlife
crowded and caged by men,
the convulsions of our democracy,
maybe fatal, revenge of the racist
patriarchy, the cancer at the core

of America, spreading again
after we'd thought we had it beaten.

I yield no quarter as fall approaches,
let every pestilence have its day,
let winter come, my favorite season,
I stand my ground as fate unfolds.

October

Once a month that grew cooler
now a hot dry season of fire-fear
earth responds to our abuse
with equal disregard
for human and innocent life.

Year End

December arrives, and not too soon
This bad year will come to an end.
It's a month to enjoy in any event
With its mists and longest night
Some rain with luck, some bright clear days
And then another year begins, and winter
In earnest, the finest season in California.
The evils that plagued the year before
Will run their course of course, but we
May renew in the bareness of January
The noblest human hope — that with care,
And luck, and some skill,
We can make things better not worse.

On the Mountain V

Many crows up top this time, more
than fifty, not making a racket like they do
in the neighborhood, just hanging around,
some on the ground, some in the trees,
some in the air. A little clicking was
the only sound I heard them make, except
for twice when one flew so close
I caught the wingbeats. They kept a wary eye
on me as I made the rounds, station to station,
absorbing the views below and the sounds
of the wind in the firs and the bays, of the surf
down on Stinson, a symphony of *shh* chords,
each different, coming variously to ear
from wing, fir, bay, and wave,
fitting accompaniment to the panoramas
of ocean, coast, bay, bridges, cities, mountains.
In the hush it was as if the crows,
gangsters though they are, held
a reverence for the place akin to mine.

Not That Into Us

The nation lies in ruins, mountains and rivers remain.
TU FU

Tu's rivers have been dammed, his mountains
denuded as elsewhere, but nature's indifference
pervades serenely. The arrogant child humankind
will strut and fret and wipe out fellow kinds
and eventually its own, but she is fine with bacteria.
All the time in the world for something different
to emerge. It's good to bear witness, like Tu, but don't
expect sympathy. Sometimes I look at drifting clouds
and terror stirs at cold heaven passing by.

What Is

*Reality is frighteningly superior to all fiction, all fable,
all divinity, all surreality.*
ARTAUD

Artaud, of course, was insane
but maybe a madman sees best the folly
of our fond imaginings, how weak
they are arrayed against the real,

the massive flux, the woven merciless
flow that cannot be reversed.
Mortally immersed, we see only
slices that slip through windows,

glimpse patterns but only peer so far.
The passing pictures are what we have
of the world, along with our sole
possession—the body, the self, the strange

familiar unit that learns, learns until
it yields at last to entropy, the king of time.

Apperception

"A maximum of appearances in close correlation
with unknown realities"—that's what the old Monet
told his friend Clemenceau he was working on.
Apt, for perception is projection produced
by the brain and rapidly tuned in accord
with the signals arriving, to correlate
with the world around as closely as
the apparatus can manage—illusions composed
to meet human needs in a world all too real,
and all too impossible to know. The beauty
is a gift, and the business of the artist, and surely
Monet made a maximum of his appearances.

I look up for the waxing crescent
in the evening sky, and there it is,
dependable, now cruising above
clouds combed out like lovely hair.
Down toward the horizon a bank
of curly clouds begins to ignite
as the sun descends....
All a matter of perspective of course.
The pictures provided by the eye
and the brain are not just illusions.
They are representations
of an implacable reality
and though they give us
but a version, it serves us well.
I love paintings, I'll be going
out of my way to see some soon,
but no painting can compare
to the scenes the brain
provides, thickening the moment
by moment shifting, giving us
something to see that seems real.

Only I

"This is not the moon
and this is not the springtime
that were here last year.
Only I remain the same,"
said Narihira, the lover,

finding no one there
when he came back to the place
where a promise was made.
She was elsewhere, and maybe
he deserved that, who can say.

But he had a point—
our little self is battered
by time and finally
dies like every living thing
but meanwhile stubbornly stands

on its square inch,
holding against the current
of the flowing world,
playing a role for itself
and its fellows, to the end.

Ariwara no Narihira, 825–880 CE

The Extent of It

Only nothing is infinite

Angenga

Lone-walker, that's me
often now, to my delight
everyone in the end.

Trails

Mine don't reach the back country any more,
not with these knees. Now all my paths are beaten
by thousands of human feet, year after year.
In beautiful places, sure, and uncrowded
on weekdays, but thoroughly worn—and that's fine,
I'm one of many after all, and the further I go
the closer I get to the commonest destination.
Why shouldn't the way be well-trodden?

One of the great things about walking a beach
is that there's no trail there. All the footprints
are erased by the sea, over and over again.

Boink!

When it comes down to the very end
When neural curtains close
I think I know what happens then
The TV's off, it's all zeroes
And after that I'm pretty sure
We won't be worried anymore.

Problem Is It Makes a Mess

Belmonte, the great bullfighter,
on hearing that his friend Hemingway
had blown his brains out, said
"Well done." And, they say
when Belmonte learned
that his heart and lungs
were riddled with disease,
so that smoking, drinking, riding,
and making love were forbidden,
he chose some cigars, took
two bottles of his favorite wine,
saddled his best horse, and
rode out to his ranch, where—
these final pleasures exhausted—
he blew his brains out.

Solstice Ferry

The lowest sun, dimmed by pewter fog
in the sky to the south, still glints and dances
on the waters of the bay, dark waters bearing
the ferry on its regular path to and from
the city where, in restaurants old and new
people celebrate the last day of the year
according to the sun. According to the sun
its due for regular trips up and down the sky,
we celebrate the circulation of the blood
and the glimmering thoughts that dance
for the fortunate living, who know one day
will be the last, and one last trip will take us
to the darkness of nothing, infinite respite.

2023

On the Mountain VI

Delayed by illness till Friday,
last chance this week, so I make
the drive through Mill Valley again
onto the ridge, into the forest
emerging in dense fog up top.

I know by heart the coasts
that lie behind this blank mist,
and silhouettes of tree and rock
do not conceal details of groves
and boulders held in memory.

This Egret

Patrols the docks in a basin I frequent,
stalking something. Hunting behavior
to a T, the coiled neck, the carefully
placed articulated feet, the peering.
Here it's into water too deep for spearing,
but mostly around the planked platforms
and into the boats beside them.

Perhaps "this" egret is more than one
and it's a behavior of egrets
to patrol docks—but I don't think so.
I think this egret found a bounty
on the dock one time—half a hot dog,
maybe. A flavor not to be forgotten.
And ever since, might as well check.

On the Ridge

The air above this bony spur is home
To hawk and buzzard, kite and crow,
Swift and hummingbird, and I come
To join them on the height, where down below

The ancient river now holds ocean tides,
And the glimmering bay embraces cities,
Islands, bridges, ships, piers. The eye abides
In this great lake of light and air, at ease.

I clamber down the flank and turn my feet
Into a craggy knife-edged other-world
Where slabs of serpentine like dragons' teeth
Stand in ranks of weathered blades, crazily gnarled.

They draw the eye into their wildernesses —
Lichens, crevices, caves ... small fastnesses.

West Marin

This time of year some trees declare themselves
in elegant branchings, spare against the evergreens—
redwood, pine, fir, cedar—who keep their cloaks,
here and there torn or threadbare. The hills are green
as Ireland and studded with stone. It's a mix
of ranchers, rich people, old hippies, working folk,
proprietors, artists . . . and us tourists of course.

In town there's a crazy guy, a regular,
who spouts incoherently across from the bookstore
reporting the voices in his head, which are not
interesting. But then, neither are some of the books.

On the way home, after walking beaches
with elephant seals and birds, surf cascading tier on tier
as far as we can see, and elk in the uplands,

we drive through town again and there's the loon
at his station, but quiet because an old guy has him
engaged in conversation. A respite, and that guy
is making an effort to reach a fellow human.
The street is spared the raving for a time.
The trees, green hills, and stones don't care.

Elephant Mountain

Now I see them. For years
I scanned that crest, looking
for an elephant profile.

But today five or so
matriarchs look west
from the mountain front.

Broad foreheads,
sloping trunks, ears laid back
in the watersheds.

They supervise, side by side,
the town, the bay, the ridge,
and all who see their faces.

Point Reyes Station

Drake's Beach

I'm here around a dozen times a year
and it's always different. This time
there's a new lagoon on the beach
lapping against the bluff where
there used to be sand, beloved
by elephant seals. We walk around
this new feature to reach the shore,
the usual gentle waves, and find
piles of purple along the line
of the receding tide. Mussel shells?
No, by-the-wind sailors, those simple
forms of life, who seem to have committed
suicide, but surely their plan accounts
for this catastrophe. What accounts for ours?

On the Bluff

The long beach stretches out
on either side, its fishhook curve
holding the bay, placid today
with low waves forming single file
and collapsing all at once.
Through clear air beneath high fog
the pale bluff-faces gleam,
steep buttresses against the shore.
Chimney Rock, the tip of the hook, is
cleanly etched on the silver sea-surface.

On the trail back I meet
a fine young gartersnake.
A single yellow stripe runs down
her slender back, and she pauses
to regard me from her perch
in a little bush, the scales on her cheek
an elegant lucent green, like jade.

Abbotts Lagoon

On the way in a well-fed coyote
not shy at all, trotting ahead for a little
then moving just off the trail.

At the beach looking north
it's all blue and white, looking south
all molten white gold, same ceaseless surf.

On the way back a blue heron
not shy either, stock-still lagoon-side,
looking at me looking at her.

Destination

They slide up the beach
and disappear, brief bubbles
the end of a journey.

Another set forms up
and crashes down
to sink into the sand

just like the last
with a quick
whispering rustle.

Point Reyes, North Beach

On the Mountain VII

Fog just cleared on the shoulder
Still drifting in the forests below
And clinging to the treetops of my grove
As droplets on the needles
Thousands of them, each brilliant
With its trove of sunlight.

Early at the Mission

Here ahead of time for the concert
I wander the borders of the plaza, bright
With morning sun, fountain splashing in light.
I keep to the colonnades, an introvert
Shunning the gathering crowd, and in this shade
My thoughts turn to the ancient misery of this place,
So many native souls enslaved, no trace
Of them now, even the walls and roofs they made
Have fallen and been rebuilt. But the old cruelty
However kind the intent may have been, lingers
Here where in time I take my place in line
And enter the nave with the rest of the elderly gentry.
There tortured Christ looks down, while skillful fingers
Weave keyboard harmonies, Bach's design.

Carmel

Dawn at Carmel River

After the usual ramble over the headland
I walk down the road to the wastewater
plant. A bunker low on the bank, it stands
between me and the river, slow here
as the lagoon. The east lightens.
Birds stir, flapping and sculling and calling.
I take it in and turn, boots crunching
the rocky dirt road. My shadow heightens,
zooming ahead as the morning light
shines low at my back, casting my form
in the middle of the path, all out of size.
Legs loom impossibly long, a short slight
torso perched on them, and on the top, forlorn
and tiny, a little head rides surprised.

So Happened

My timing was good, I thought, climbing
the headland at dawn, looking down
on the old lagoon. Only a few birds
this time, but everything clear, winter's edge
persisting into early spring. First flowers
along the path, quiet arms of the river holding
marshes, but then at the top, the perfect spot
for watching sunrise, another guy slipped in
ten yards ahead of me, taking the choice nook.

Well, I thought, how many times
have you stood in that place (and never seen
another person)—maybe today you'll find
something different in the passage of dawn.
So musing I made my way down the trail
the other had climbed up, and when I came
to the unpaved road, there was a cat
trotting toward me, absorbed in feline thought
ten yards away, another morning fellow.

Took me an instant to identify
the short tail, bearded cheeks, spots and stripes
of a bobcat, a young one. He startled,
leapt, dodged right, dodged left, then turned
to run down the road and into the bushes
by the wastewater plant on the river.
And so indeed my timing was good
a bobcat on a birthday is a gift
sometimes the current catches you just right.

Carmel River, 3.27.21

Otters

Five otters out in the surf
off Rabbit Ears Rock
at dawn—two adults
and three young. The grown-ups
are busy with breakfast,
diving, bringing up mussels,
flipping to float on their backs,
pounding the shells on the rocks
they put on their chests—
the cracking sounds reach shore.
One pup wanders around
as the waves pass by
and the other two play—
diving then popping up
face to face for a bout
of sparring, forepaws flying,
then doing it again.
Remarkable behaviors
in these creatures
fitted to their briny home,
and the play—to think
it's a regular feature
of every mammal childhood—
it's a perfect ponder
(to borrow from Toots).

Ancient Harvester

It's long, red, and mysteriously configured.
Two long bins sit side by side in back,
open at the end. A compartment in the middle
has a vertical post and lateral pipe fixtures,
then in front there's the seat on the left,
the steering wheel and gearshift,
plus another lever. No roof. Engine compartment in front.
Maybe it's not a harvester... fire truck?

Year by year it slowly sinks in the bark litter
of the eucalyptus grove. The tires rot, a fender falls off,
the paint flakes and fades, the rust spreads.
The creeping decrepitude of old machinery
is a spectacle of a special kind.
The old way of life is gone but a relic persists,
more enduring than the human uses it served,
outliving its people in gradual disintegration.

River

It's down there in its thicket, running
all the time, not just when glimpsed from the bridge
cruising by at fifty miles an hour
early in the morning, when the rising sun
briefly reflects the rippling current.

Unseen it's there, flowing in place
whether or not it rises in memory.
The river is there, wherever you may be.

Red Abalone

Just a baby's shell picked up
At the north end of Monastery Beach.

Inch and a half on the long side
Four holes in the selenizone

Cast four little odd moons
On my desk beneath the lamp.

The whorl, the irridescence
Are on this flashy side

But every now and then
I flip it over to see the rough

Red shell that faced
The rough ocean world

Then the four holes
Are dark and remind me

That the baby did not live
To grow and seal them.

Who knows why? Nature
Proposes and disposes.

Cavalry

When you see them
Plunging down the slopes
Of green and blue
White manes flying back
Hooves pounding up foam
Rising again in miniature
To charge the beach
Shoulder to shoulder

Then you remember
Poseidon was a god of horses.

Carmel River State Beach

On the Mountain VIII

First rains of November
have set green blades
in the earth, and brought
the mosses to life on rocks
and tree trunks — under
morning sun they glow
a richer emerald.

No one else on the trails
and this is how I like it
alone with my thoughts
and routines, fashioned
to suit my purposes
no compromises up here
on the mountain with sights
in and out, near and far.

Clipper Cove

Down from the bus on the bridge
sailboats rest on glittering beds
nets of gold spread over the harbor
slow-shifting patterns of late afternoon.

Polarized sunglasses, my prescription,
break up the glare into water-glints
flecks in the bright sun sheen.
I bought them for fishing, to catch

the twitch of the trout beneath
the surface. But I don't fish these days
these years that slide down-river
banks crowded with my kind, it puts me off.

So my lenses catch the light off the bay—
coins buried in a chest, now turned up
in a nook of the whale-road, the river-end,
the world-wrapping, tear-salty, boat-wounded sea.

Driving In

Startling the state of the forest
So many dead trees, tall tawny foliage
Done in by drought and beetles
So many acres blistered by fire
                    lie bare.

I who once wandered these mountains
On trail and off, finding ways
Through forests and over passes
Sleeping by lakes and streams
                    or on ledges,

Am on my way to a fine old hotel
In the valley, knees too creaky now
To carry a pack, country within
Dotted with dead trees, dappled with
                    barren slopes.

The Spiders

The spiders will come
After I'm gone
They'll spin their webs on the porch
And no one will sweep them away.

Oh someone will come
To sweep them away
One of your sons or perhaps
A new buyer, eager with broom.

No buyer or son
Would chase them like me
With long bamboo for high eaves
Weekly sweeping away.

Well spiders will come
Long after we're gone
Spinning webs freely
On eaves high and low.

There's comfort in that
They'll have their way
When ours has run out.
They're an old tribe.

Take comfort where you can
The spiders do not care
They spin as they please
On eaves high and low.

A Full Moon Through Binoculars

There's a node
> behind the rabbit's tail
>> beside the man's mustache.

This belly swelling
> into space has a navel.
>> It almost seems

Like some cold child
> of silver stone
>> might burst into the sky.

Carmel River State Beach, 1.11.09

A Dream

"Sufficient unto the day
are the pleasures thereof."

I woke to that refrain
knowing it wasn't right.

Upon reflection, realized
that "evil" is sufficient.

But the dream was a good one—
looking out our closet window

from the second floor,
I beheld a tiny mannequin

reclining in an apple blossom,
at exemplary ease,

a human form fashioned
from wood and wire.

I'd been admiring
a piece of street art

on a telephone pole
in Linden Alley—

one wood-and-wire
model poised to jump

from the top, three more
already tumbling down.

Sufficient unto the day
are the pleasures thereof.

And the evil.

Asilomar

Heavy fog and a night chorus of frogs
in the lagoon by the beach. I approach
and they fall silent, resume when I stop,

so step by halting step I come
to the dark water's edge and listen.

Then on to the boardwalk above the dunes
where the breakers repeat their roar,
white bundles emerging from blackness,

endless expression of the sea
with never a care for human presence.

Pausing at the footbridge on the way back
I try to catch a murmur from the creek below
under the mumble of the waves

and the moans of passing cars
and the frogs downstream.

Do I hear a current whisper
beneath me in the dark? Not sure.
I walk up the path toward the road.

Tomorrow I visit two loved ones
near death. Walk now and listen in the dark.

Summer 2011; 4.20.18

January Thought

Bony fingers of the trees
    under the streetlight

Reach for the sun
    during the night

Patterns developed
    in this place

To meet the limits
    of the space

Nets of consciousness
    grow that way

Explaining the things
    we saw yesterday.

On the Mountain IX

This time the fog is closing in
just as I arrive—I catch
but a glimpse of the east bay
from the ridge line trail.

So I take the interior loop.
It's not pristine—the trails here
are less trampled, but still trodden
and with my usual plastic bag

I pick up after someone's
defecation. Not too bad, it's
been a few months, just the paper,
but—what is it with people?

I visit my madrones in the mist
off the trail—they've shed their bark
and the naked trunks are pale.
Many seedlings sprout around them

after last year's wonderful winter.
Maybe a succession is underway.
The poison oak is bright red.
In autumn I love this place.

Autumn Lights

Walking up Virginia across from the station
November sun slants low from the east
Flows around the forms of the patient
Commuters lined up on Sacramento, seized
By the jaws of the job and the carpool.
Between these wights blink flashing lights
From a cruiser across the street. He's pulled
Someone over and likes to flaunt his might
But distracts the drivers approaching —
One plows through the crosswalk, I pause.
Autumn is here in its slow decline, its dim
Hours, its sudden small slippages, cause
To remember the year is sliding past
Joining the others, leaving us fast.

End of November

Now the season has fully turned
and hangs like ripened fruit.
In the cool stillness my heart yearns
for another change, a further tilt
of the Earth away from the Sun …
Bring me bare branches, long cold nights,
rain, wind, gray storms, big surf,
clean streets, clear skies. Winter's truth.

12.19.22

Coming out of the library
head full of reading
it's dusk at 4:15, gray sky
and bare branches as I walk
downhill, past Moffitt, past
Life Sciences, past
the Eucalyptus Grove,
then by the brain research
building to Berkeley Way, and
on to the roads home.

Dad's birthday,
and it's exhilarating,
his favorite time of year
and mine beginning.

Passage

January, you're leaving me desolate again
your bare branches soon to swell with buds
your cold clarity yielding to warm vapors
it always happens, good times quickly pass
the current constantly carries us helpless
away from what we love, into something else.

The plum doesn't know
How its branches are arranged
To show off white blossoms
In February's dark

End of February

I get suspicious when it's this good—
lots of rain, and the other day
a scatter of hailstones on my walk
sending a shiver of anxiety since
I left without a jacket. Some early plum
blossoms are gone already, and some
late bloomers are yet to declare—
it's all good, but of course there'll be
the change of seasons, and a reversion
to the mean. Foolish to think otherwise.

On the Mountain X

Miles on the way up—*Kind of Blue*
Herbie on the way down—*River*
Traditional tunes for a traditional trip.

Trail maintenance at Station One
Wind in the firs, a little trash
To pick up, not too bad.

Trail from One to Two
The usual eerie views
Of forests alive on the slopes.

More maintenance at Two—
Satisfaction. Drake's Bay bluffs
Just visible. Surf surges on Stinson.

Three, the first glimpse
Of winter sun on the gulf
Through bay leaves and branches

Massive expanse
Of spreading wave patterns
On the ebb of the tide.

On the way to Four,
City and East Bay appear
And on the bench attention

Is commanded by the sprawl
Of the view below. Here
I see people over at Five

A mom and a kid with two dogs.
They take a trail below,
I go to Five, where mushrooms

Poke out of the fallen oak—
Chanterelles? Right color, wrong shape.
More maintenance on the trail

Leading up from the east
And as I head out to the west
A guy comes up that trail.

Follow the ridgeline
Back to the car, where another guy
Greets me and asks

If there's anything good for dinner—
He thinks I'm a forager. I tell him I'm not,
But I am in a way.

The Rain

A rainy day in a California December
can take you back to a California boyhood
in the home, with books, everything you need
to nurture roots, the rain on the roof
the rhythm, your thoughts the melody.

Surely the rain will bring poems, you think,
listening and remembering in the gray light.

Gnomon

On the day of its northernmost rising
I went to see the sun caught in the lantern
atop the bell tower. The way to the long shadow
led to the south porch of Bancroft Library
from there the tall stone shaft soared up
out of treetops, and at the tip of the spire
the lantern, itself topped and surrounded
by sets of smaller spiking spires
shone bright with concentrated sunlight.
"Fiat Lux," I said, in that time and place.

6.21.23, 9:00 AM

Buddhas

Our little buddha's picturesque,
bright leaves of maple and persimmon
nestle round his folded legs.
The Buddha's long gone in the void
where everyone goes, but he
left thoughts that comfort people—
so his statue sits beneath our maple.

Green and Gold

High up in these poplars
I planted, late sun
in early summer glows gold
over green leaves.

The trees roar with wind
as fog moves in
gray fringes closing
on blue afternoon.

Green and gold
toss and turn
fifty feet in the air
above my chair.

No saving the scene
everything passes—
wind in the trees, colors,
rocking chairs.

Some crispness
in the moment tho.

West Berkeley

Trains blow their whistles at each street crossing.
At night and early in the morning
the bellows carry over the neighborhood
bringing with them an early memory
from another place by the bay, where
my three-year-old self would run down the sidewalk
in front of the row of apartments
and grasp the chain link fence to watch the trains
go by—sometimes an engineer would blow
the whistle, just to please a fascinated child.

Surely the Rain

Red Pine is one of my favorite translators
from the Chinese, but when he has Tu Fu
say "surely the rain will bring poems"
I think he misses the meaning. Other versions
make it pretty clear that Tu is on a boat,
with a party going on, and it's about to rain
so he needs to hurry to finish writing
his poems. No doubt the Chinese lends itself
to Red's phrasing, though, and he frames
a beautiful thought. Now rain, always welcome
in California, brings that line to mind
every time. And also my friend Tom
who quoted it to me many years ago,
before the melanoma came and took his life …
Yesterday was a lovely rainy day
to think of Tu Fu, and of Tom.

Home three days now
and still missing it—
southwestern rim of Mono Basin
high desert and craggy peaks
aspens brighter gold each day
clarity in the features of the land
in garrulous creeks and glittering lakes—
the mind tunes to the place.

Uno Día Más

And it's by the bay, with shimmering light
on the water at the turn of low tide, and birds
and boats on the move, and myself swung along
with all of it, caught afloat but with the wheel
still in my hands, the craft not sunk yet.

Translations

Book I, Ode XI

Horace

Don't ask what end the gods have granted us—
that knowledge is forbidden, my friend, and don't try
guessing with magic numbers. Better abide whatever comes,
whether this winter that's wearing out the sea against the rocks
is one of many more, or the last we'll see. Come to your senses,
open a bottle of wine, and since our time is short
trim back the term of hope. As we've spoken, jealous age
has gained some ground—so take today, trust little in tomorrow.

Book I, Ode XVIII

Horace

Plant no tree before you start the sacred vines
in that soft soil outside the city walls. The god of wine
decrees that those who spurn his cup shall suffer all hardships,
and there's no better cure for the constant bite of worry.
After wine, who natters on about his troubles in the army
or his poverty? Who instead doesn't sing your praises,
Father Bacchus, and yours, lovely Venus? And yet,
those who abuse the gifts of the vine could learn a lesson
from the Centaurs' drunken wedding brawl, and from
that greedy tribe of Thrace, who so displeased the god of ecstasy
by viewing right and wrong along the lines of their desires.
I'd never rouse you against your will, Bacchus, so fine but so feral,
nor ever bring to light your mysteries, hidden by many leaves.
Hold back the wild drums and horns; they're only followed by
blind love of Self, and empty Glory lifting high its head,
and feckless Trust revealing secrets, clear as glass.

Book I, Ode XXXIV

after Horace

Never one for piety, adept at rationalization,
I figure no one up there cares, it's best to live
    a good life by your own lights,
    causing no harm, enjoying friends.

Just now though, thunder rolling through
a clear blue sky reminded me—there are those
    surprises, things that shake
    the earth, make the waters jump,

break the everyday, and scare up superstitions.
The old fears and faiths have power, no use
    denying that. And however free
    your thinking, some disaster

can pull you down, or put a fool in a high place
to fill your days with aggravation, or worse. It seems
    Fate takes a harsh delight
    playing favorites, stripping victims.

Book II, Ode I

Horace

Pollio, it's work full of dangerous risks
you've taken up, the story of our civil strife,
    the causes, the phases, the terrible mistakes,
        the games of Fate,

the grave pacts between leaders,
the blades coated with blood, still unavenged.
    You're stepping on ashes while fire
        still smolders beneath.

For a while now the theater has missed
your tragic muse. Let it be soon, once you've set
    the record straight, that you
        return to the stage,

and to your post as eminent counsel
defending clients, advising the Senate,
    resting on laurels earned
        in military triumph.

But now you fill my ears with moaning horns
and blaring clarions; now I see weapons flaring,
    kindling terror in shying horses,
        in riders' faces.

Now it seems I hear the captains shout,
magnificently grimed with battle dust;
    now all the land is conquered—but for
        grim Cato's soul.

Juno and the other gods who favored Africa
but could not stop us there, have offered up
    the victors' grandsons at the tomb
        of the enemy king.

What field has not been glazed with Roman blood,
its graves the signs of our unholy wars,
    proclaiming the fall of the West
        to those who hate us?

What pool, what stream has not been fed
by our tears? What sea not stained
    by our corpses? What coast not touched
        by our gore?

But now, my Muse, let's not forget the jokes,
trying to sing these heavy lamentations.
    Come seek with me a lighter tune,
        a lovelier place.

Book II, Ode XV

Horace

Sailors caught on the open sea
when black clouds hide the moon
and block the guiding starlight,
    ask the gods for relief.

Tribes seek relief from battle,
empires from armament, relief
that cannot be bought, my rich friend,
    with gems, or gold, or robes.

Neither treasure nor power of office
Dispels the troubles crowding the mind
or the miseries that flit about
    beneath a paneled ceiling.

It's good to live with little; the sleep
of a man whose father's salt-cellar
shines on a plain table is not broken
    by neediness or fear.

Why do we try so hard for so much,
in our brief time? Why do we go to lands
warmed by a foreign sun? Who escapes his country
    and himself too?

Warping worry boards the best boats
and rides with companies of cavalry,
swifter than deer, swifter than the wind
    that drives the clouds.

The mind can be happy for a while,
refusing to dwell on what's beyond,
tempering bitterness with a smile, but
    no blessing is unmixed.

Death took bright Achilles quickly,
endless age diminished Tithonus,
and maybe time will offer me
    what it denies to you.

Choice cattle bellow in your fields,
chariot horses whinny for you,
wool steeped twice in purple dye
    drapes your shoulders.

Fate, no lie, has granted me
a little land, a little feeling
for Greek verse, and a scorn
    for the jealous crowd.

Book II, Ode XXI

Horace

You were born with me when Manlius was consul
and now, whether it's quarrels or quips you harbor,
    complaints or crazy love
      or soft sleep, my good bottle,

forget your plans for saving that choice vintage,
worthy to serve on a special occasion. Come out tonight—
    Corvinus has requested
      a mellower bibulation!

Steeped though he is in Socratic discourse,
he won't be too swollen to absorb your bounty;
    even the virtuous Cato, they say,
      was often warm with wine.

You gently bend the spirit, where usually it's stiff;
you open up the secrets and the worries of the wise
    with laughter loosened by
      the god who sends us reveling.

You bring back hope to anxious minds,
and lend the hearts of poor men strength and courage;
    with you, they lose their fear
      of angry kings and armored soldiers.

You come to us with Freedom, and glowing Love
if She agrees to visit, and the Graces, linked together
    in the lamplight, till the sun
      returns to put the stars to flight.

Book III, Ode XXII

Horace

Diana, Lady of mountains and forests,
Who saves young mothers from death in childbirth
When called three times—goddess of three realms,
    The Wild, the Moon, and Hades—

I'm making this pine leaning over my house your shrine,
So that every New Year's Day I can take a boar
Who thinks he's about to give me a sidelong slash
    And offer his blood to you.

Book IV, Ode VII

Horace

The snow is gone, the grasses are back in the fields
    and the leaves in the trees,
Earth rolls through her changes and the rivers drop,
    now running in their banks.
The Graces will venture out with the Nymphs, undressed
    to lead their choirs.
The year, and the hour that steals away, warn us not
    to hope for immortality.
Cold winds turn warm, then summer tramples spring
    and itself goes under,
As apple-bearing autumn brings the harvest in again,
    then numb cold returns.
New moons grow back what old ones lose
    but when we slip below
to join the Roman kings of old—pious, rich, and good—
    we're all dust and shadow.
Who knows if the gods will let us add tomorrows
    to the sum of our todays?
Remember, what you give your friendly self escapes
    the clutches of your heirs.
Once you go down, and great Minos passes judgment
    on you, nothing,
not your family, not your eloquence, not your faith,
    can bring you back.

Jade Flower Palace

Tu Fu

The fast river bends, the long wind
Rushes through pines. Gray rats scuttle
Under ancient tiles. What lord built
This place beside the cliffs, then
Left it to ruin? In dark rooms facing north,
Green ghost fires. On broken pavements,
Scouring waves. Nature's thousand pipes
Are the music now, fall colors the decoration,
The beautiful ladies are yellow dust
No trace of their powders and paints.
The courtiers and golden carriage
Are gone—only a stone horse is left
On a grave mound. Sorrow comes
As I sit on the grass, writing this song.
The journey lies ahead, but who lives long?

To Wei Pa

Tu Fu

Lives have lapsed since last we met,
Stars at opposite ends of the sky, we two,
But tonight we share the lamplight.
Youth and strength, how brief they were!
Now our hair is thin and gray ...
We ask after old friends — half of them
Are ghosts, shock and sorrow
Pierce us through. How could we have known
It would be twenty years until
I came to your house again?
You weren't married last time I saw you
Now a row of boys and girls
Comes merrily in to greet their father's friend,
Asking him where he's been, but before
I can answer you send them off
To set out wine and a meal.
Spring onions cut in this night's rain,
New rice steamed with yellow millet.
You say "we see each other so rarely!"
And pour out cups of wine, ten times.
Still I'm not drunk — it's old friendship
that fills me now. Tomorrow hills and waters
Will separate us again — them
And the endless business of the world.

Coming Home at Night

Tu Fu

Midnight, passing tigers on the road, home now
In the mountain dark, family asleep in the house

Beside me the dipper slips down to the river
A bright star hangs above, huge in the empty sky

Holding a candle in the courtyard, I call for torches
A gibbon startles and cries in the canyon

My white head is old and tired but I dance and sing too
Up late with my goosefoot cane—can't beat this!

Facing Snow

Tu Fu

So many new ghosts from the war
An old man can but chant his sorrow

Broken clouds bottom the evening sky
Wind whips snow swirls into frenzies

The ladle lies beside the empty jar
The stove still glows a little red

No word from neighboring districts
Grieving I sit and write in emptiness

Leaving the City
Tu Fu

Evening comes, icy icy frost
I look up and down the tall heavens

There's smoke over distant salt mines
Shadows slanting from mountain snows

Soldiers on horseback still plague the homeland
War drums sound in this far province too

Leaving the city by the river as night comes on
I return to my old friends the cawing crows

Standing Alone
Tu Fu

Empty sky above a hawk
Two white gulls on the river

Floating lazily, easy targets
They drift around aimlessly

Frost has killed the grass
But spiderwebs still hang

Heaven's loom weaves our affairs
Ten thousand sources of sorrow

At a Meeting of Rivers
Tu Fu

Yangzi and Han, I'm headed home
An old poet between Heaven and Earth
Scattered clouds in a faraway sky, like me,
Moon alone in a cold night, like me.
As the sun goes down, my mind is still agile,
As the fall wind blows, my illness improves.
I ride the old horse to take me back
Though he can't go far any more.

Night Thoughts Traveling
Tu Fu

Grasses bend in the wind on the banks
The boat's mast rises alone in the night

Stars drop down to the broad plain
Moonlight swirls in the great river

Poems—will they ever bring me honor?
Office—age and illness preclude me.

Drifting along here, what am I like?
A gull between heaven and earth.

Deer Park
Wang Wei

Up in the mountains
No one around
Sometimes I think
I hear voices

Sunlight slips
Between the trees
Glows green again
On mosses overhead

Fragment
Li Po

I wake from a dream to the mat and the pillow
Gone are the scenes from a moment ago
All the world's pleasures are like this
The river of events flows east to the past

Fragment

Su Tung-P'o

Don't mind the beat of the rain
    on the leaves
Think of a poem as we walk along

Staff and sandals are better
    than a saddle
No worries here, I could spend

My life in the mist and rain
    this chill spring wind
Has made my mind keen

The sun slants high on a hill up ahead
    a look behind
At bleakness, and on I go whatever the weather

The Wind

Su Tung-P'o

The invisible wind is a marvel
A thing that is felt, not known
It travels around like a prince
And wherever it goes
Grasses and trees whisper its praises

Our outing today is aimless
I greet the breeze, let the boat drift
And lift a cup to the cosmos—
How fine it is that neither it nor I
Have a care in the world for each other

On the way home through the valleys
Moonlight gleams on clouds and waters

Thoughts Passing a Farm House

Lu Yu

Reins loose, I follow the sinking sun along the river.
Whose well and threshing floor are these, behind a wicker gate?
A dog barks through the fence
The silkworms are hungry on their frames
Ten years in government have disgusted me
My distant home is dim in my dreams
Farming is better for a man
You could do worse than to die on your own land.

About the Author

Alan Archer Stephens was a judicial staff attorney for California appellate courts before he retired in 2018. His father was the Santa Barbara poet Alan Stephens. He lives in Berkeley with his wife Donna Hiraga-Stephens.

www.ingramcontent.com/pod-product-compliance
Ingram Content Group UK Ltd.
Pitfield, Milton Keynes, MK11 3LW, UK
UKHW041305180426
11947UKWH00009B/703